OFF DUTY

Katie Donovan was educated at Trinity College Dublin and the University of California at Berkeley. She has published five books of poetry with Bloodaxe Books: *Watermelon Man* (1993), *Entering the Mare* (1997), *Day of the Dead* (2002), *Rootling: New and Selected Poems* (2010) and *Off Duty* (2016). Born in 1962, she spent her childhood on a farm in Co. Wexford before moving to Dun Laoghaire, a suburb of Dublin where she still lives. She has worked as a journalist with *The Irish Times*, and as a lecturer in Creative Writing, formerly at IADT and now at NUI Maynooth.

Her work has been widely anthologised, most recently in *The Wake Forest Book of Irish Women's Poetry*, edited by Peggy O'Brien, and in *Staying Alive: real roems for unreal times*, edited by Neil Astley.

KATIE DONOVAN

Off Duty

BLOODAXE BOOKS

ISBN: 978 1 78037 316 4

First published 2016 by
Bloodaxe Books Ltd,
Eastburn,
South Park,
Hexham,
Northumberland NE46 1BS.

www.bloodaxebooks.com
For further information about Bloodaxe titles
please visit our website or write to
the above address for a catalogue.

Supported using public funding by

**ARTS COUNCIL
ENGLAND**

Cover design: Neil Astley & Pamela Robertson-Pearce.

Printed in Great Britain by Bell & Bain Limited, Glasgow, Scotland, on
acid-free paper sourced from mills with FSC chain of custody certification.

For my mother, Deborah Troop

ACKNOWLEDGEMENTS

Acknowledgements are due to the editors of the following publications in which some of these poems, or earlier versions of them, first appeared: *Banshee, Crannog, The Clifden Anthology, Cyphers, The Enchanting Verses Literary Review* (India, special Irish edition edited by Pat Cotter), *Inside History: the work of Eavan Boland*, ed. Siobhán Campbell & Nessa O'Mahony (Arlen House / Syracuse University Press, 2016), *Irish Pages, The Irish Independent, The Irish Times* and *Southword*. Also to *Sunday Miscellany*, RTE Radio One.

I am grateful to Enda Wyley for choosing 'Wish' to be part of the installation she curated at the Coombe Women and Infant's University Hospital in Dublin. This project featured six writers and was launched with a wonderful speech by our poet president, Michael D. Higgins, for International Women's Day, 2012.

CONTENTS

The Game of Sleep

Tenderly tucking,
my daughter plays
the game of sleep.
Nearly two, she loves
my old stuffed penguin best,
a mouse with a belly button,
and her new rag doll.
This favoured crew
is propped on pillows,
swathed in blankets.

She and I join in,
her curly laughing head
pressed sideways against mine,
her bottom lifted, wiggling.
Then she's off,
romping on the big bed —
the very feather and down
of her making —
she leaps and rolls and tunnels,
throws herself, chuckling,
into the cushiony give
of chequered quilt.

I tickle and trip, revelling
in her giggly mouth's cascade,
her nuzzling joy,
a gift this bed bestows,
just as her begetting here
was rose; was gold.

Hold On

No wonder women like to feed for years:
the cosy ritual is hard to sacrifice,
the little hand, resting possessively
on the industrious breast,
as it pumps the best nectar in town.
There's the gratifying feeling
of good work going on quietly,
all the better when I don't even try.
There's the knowing I can give nourishment
at any place or time. Now, just as I feel it is an art
I've mastered, the world sticks its nose in,
prizing us apart, and I must farm you out
with fussy paraphernalia –
bottles, toys, flaked food and pureed mush –
to go to work behind a desk,
my body bound like a lunatic in a cell,
the brain ticking frenetically on,
my breasts weeping in my sharp work shirt,
for you, so far away, without their comfort.

Child's Play

I blow bubbles: orbs of bluey pink
winking and teasing in airy spurts.
They reach to pinch and crush,
feet lift to stamp, little teeth chortling.
When I lie down, they flump on my belly
whooping as I cry. Having 'expired',
I sit up – alive again,
ready for 'tea', poured with serious pride
from a red pot with a yellow lid.

When I mount and wobble off,
out of practice on my old bike,
I see myself in their eyes:
a giant on a huge machine.

If I come home with tales of woe
I can picture it – what, you got hit
by a bus? Guess what happened to us!

Wish

(for Kirsten)

You walk in,
little sprite,
your skin
smooth as an egg,
big eyes
fascinated
by my lumps
and hairy places:
the kind of body
you can't conceive
of growing into.

But your tiny mermaid fold
will grow and frond
like mine,
your bottom
swell out proud
as new bread,
your nipples rise up
like raspberries
pointing at the sun.

It's all ahead of you.

Just as when
I found my mother –
a strange aquatic giant –
lounging in the bath,
with all her flesh
and wet hair floating free.
As she stood
with water streaming down,

I coveted
the balanced round of her,

not knowing
my body was only waiting
for the day
to make my wish come true.

Christmas Birds

Christmas, a mild afternoon
of 'eggball' in the garden
with two blissed out children;
all their wishes satiated,
their little hands learning
to catch and throw.
Later they run among
the eucalyptus trees,
showing their new toy birds
what it's like 'in the forest'.

Arrival

Tulip, our new cat,
surprises us on the top bunk:
four little tabbies,
slick with afterbirth,
are tongued and nudged
to feed. She cleans up,
devouring the placenta –
nutritious and neat.

Fifteen years since
I last saw this: Spring
and my Tia, still a kitten herself,
nesting in the wardrobe,
mewing with the cramps,
but knowing how to cope.

Today the wheel turns –
a new feline family comes
to enchant my daughter's bedroom.
She, Phoebe, keeps guard;
as the babies nuzzle and suck,
each fluffy scrap is named.
She can watch for hours
the drama of puckered faces
and tiny claws;
the purring of the mother,
so deep, so loud, Phoebe claims
she can feel it in her bones.

Labour

i.m. Savita Halappanavar, died 28 October 2012,
in University Hospital Galway.

Lying on my back,
because the midwife said,
I nearly turned myself
inside out, like a wrong sock,
pushing, in a panic.
Not till the second baby's time
did I clue in to gravity,
the anarchic success
of stride and swing.

I was biddable,
until when they began
to wheedle me
with talk of an episiotomy,
to scold and wither
when I refused the knife.
The small tear she made
shouldering out
was nothing
compared to their plan
of slicing me
like some vegetal pod.

They prefer the regimental
recline and push, it fits
their schedule, followed
by the slitting, and after –
the ward too busy for the breast –
whispering to our insecurities:
'Just use the bottle.'

Tell us when and how
it suits the hospital
to do our work.
Lay us down, so you can see,
and we can't push.
Cut us so our yells
hiss out as air,
dismiss our fears
and cover up
the damage and mistakes,
that leave us hurting,
ashamed, incapable
or dead.

Sinking

In Texas, in 2000, Andrea Yates drowned
her five children in the bath.

I bore five babies for God.
I loved their round faces,
shining like candles,
but the weight of their innocence
was too great
for my one pair
of woman's hands.
I felt myself sinking
so I saved my nest of chicks,
washing their sweet breath
back to God,
one by one, in the bath.
I pushed their trusting heads
beneath the water.
They never stirred,
they knew their mother's touch
would set them on their path,
floating off to heaven.

As for me –
I was free.

The Journey; the Destination

You stand, spare, lean legs in baggy pants,
the plans for the trip upon you now,
a few hours left to sleep, no packing done.
There is a furrow between your eyes,
there is something you have forgotten.
It will haunt you as you fly.
There will be many crossings,
each time you will feel closer to your goal,
each time it will outwit you,
fingering your passport, paralysed.

The night before your father left,
he was afflicted so. Your mother slept,
you tight in her womb, her bags ready.
She knew where she was due –
far from post-war Germany,
in bright, beckoning America.
Your father used up hours,
unable to gather a semblance of his life
into one suitcase: his studies,
his teenaged soldierhood,
fleeing the enemy through the snow.
Your mother wanted what was for her a home.
He was stepping into the unknown.
Three months later you were born.

You still dream of a homecoming
in Germany, America, Denmark, Estonia –
the many countries where your family roamed.
You seek them out like apples that just might
be stuck back on the tree, a tree that you could climb
and build a house in.

Poem to a Sleeping Man

I breakfast on air and dew,
with the tumultuous birds
this summer morning.
Then I come back to you
sprawled central on our bed,
elbows ready to pin my hip
to the seesaw edge.

How I have feasted
on your brown neck ruffed with curls,
the length of your muscled frame.
Now I'm grumpily aware
of the buzz of your snore,
the taint of your night breath.

So much of your interior resists
the reach of my sleuthing arts,
including your unspeaking love,
which my parched searchlight
must take on trust – does it survive my storms
behind the cooler weather of your brow?

When the circle of our domestic hum
grows wearisome, you disappear
into the remnant of your single life,
and I cling, weeping on the wreck
of what I wanted in romantic love,
wondering if it – whatever *it* was meant to be –
has flown this coop, to hover over couples
whose beds are scented with the sensual dance
misplaced in all our petty rounds
of work and feed and clean;

or maybe I'm at last a member
of the vast majority, who do their daily best,
before finding a place to snooze
until the wakening up.

Shell

Empty and cold
I lie on the dry surface
my pink exposed
my spines crested.
I miss the water –
the enveloping element –
the cartwheel of the waves,
the caress of the undertow.
How a soft creature
would track my hollow,
make in me a nest.
My colours shine there.
Here in the air
I am dull, brittle;
all I can offer
when I am held
is a rustling mockery
of tides. It is not real,
it is a trick
of their strange
convoluted ears,
yet they smile
as if they know my secret,
as if, through me,
they can really touch the sea.

The Drowning Elephant

On 14 August 2002, the city of Prague flooded,
including the zoo.

Don't believe them
when they said
I'd been put down,
and died in comfort.
I was still breathing
when the helicopter came
to film my drowning –
no rope to pull me free,
just the manic buzz
of the propeller,
as they watched
my frantic dance
to keep my head up.

Be warned
you who are the pets
of this fickle world:
for thirty years
I was the toast of Prague,
they came to marvel
at my bulk,
and I entertained
as best I could
behind the bars.

Then the floods came
and where was Noah
when I needed him?
Behind the camera, shooting
as my trusting trunk
lifted fruitlessly above the brim.

The river sucks my breath.
May the water swallow me,
and sweep away
the hollow-hearted city,
with all its poaching lenses,
and carry my dizzy bursting head
to the bloated sleep
of the drowned.

Oh mammoth brothers, I come to you,
tusks and trunk aloft.

The Next Exit

Anger rides my fat lip, goading it
to spit the rough words you hate.
Because you're ill, I now can't spill
the vitriol the way I did.
You never could quite take
the dose I handed out,
and now you're spared the trip.
My teeth ache to their roots
while you idle in your lane,
until the next exit.

Still Well

I am the woman who is still well,
owed a year of sleep,
raw from her father's funeral,
but still well. Watching over
the children, the house, her work.
Everyone says how well she looks,
to make her feel better – clearly
she hasn't time to groom in a mirror,
she wants to make sure her babies eat,
and not too much of the junk they're offered
by kind people, thinking it's such a treat.
At bedtime she struggles to brush decay
from the small reluctant teeth. Falls asleep
as their warm bodies nestle in her arms,
then jolts awake, jaw clamped tight.
When at last she's settled for the night,
he lies beside her, slumbrous.
Next week he'll go for two months
to treat his illness – chemo in Germany.
She fears the depradations
the poisonous 'cure' will bring,
but staying home is not an option,
with the certain loss of his salivary gland,
given the outdated Irish machines.
She looks forward to his leaving,
at least it will end the sham
of him being here but not,
the endless calls and explanations,
him off for hours in health food shops,
locking her out when she tries to talk.
He's ill, she's well – she must watch her tongue,
it's hard when he ignores the children,
but there are days she's staggered to the core,

by how far apart they are, and how
this has been happening for a year or more,
is it really so different from before?

Gluing Up

Just when I wondered how
I'd stretch myself to carry
all that was laid out for me to bear,
just then it came, the droop
in my white cat's head,
too much like her mother's to ignore.
Then too, my first real stir
was the dip in the dappled face,
the shoulders tight, the breathing sore –
how had I not been quicker to see her fail?
Too wrapped up in late pregnancy,
and now again her daughter's illness comes
when all's adrift already – every solid thing
I could have sworn was there beneath my hand –
gone. Somehow until now I had been keeping
the frets at bay, as my love does battle
with his cancer, far away. But this one,
who claimed from kittenhood a place
upon my knee, when she nestles to me now
is thin and wan, reminding me
of my father, in his coffin, only months ago.

This is how I break, like unbreakable glass
that's hit with just one more random blow,
pieces of me scatter, dots of ice,
all over the kitchen floor. Until, that is,
I must glue up, give the cat her pills,
piece together my rotten teeth,
attempt to start the ailing car –
I have two children to collect,
to bathe, entertain and feed.

High Rack

End of the year, the line, my tether.
He can scarcely eat or speak
in far off Germany,
the children have coughs and fevers,
and the white cat suffers her leukemia
by losing her appetite.

At the eleventh hour I get inspired,
try slivers of succulent lamb
which the cat suddenly adores.
The phone rings:
it's him, slurring whispers
of reassurance that he's fine,
the hospital's on holiday
so no more radiation.

Upstairs the children sleep
cossetted in my bed, breathing
easily at last. I call my father's wife
greeting the New Year on her own.
We remember my dad,
the big baritone of his song,
knocking at the door with a coal in his hand,
blowing on his pipes for Hogmanay.

Recovery is so slow
it barely seems to move,
and yet the progress
a few days on is clear.
He is eating eggs,
getting ready to come home.
The Lazarus cat enjoys reprieve
by guzzling bellyfuls

of everything she sees.
The children help me
hang the washing on the high rack,
small arms lifting for the hanging slats.

They've seen me leaping
to pull down a sock, and now
it's a new game. Flushed faces
turned up, their little mouths
are laughing: I am their giantess,
all breasts and belly and legs.
I hope I can stand this test
until their father is strong again.

Tears Naturelle

Tears Naturelle
is the label on the bottle
prescribed as a remedy
for my chronic dry eyes.
After your throat
parched tight
and you couldn't eat,
my eyes dried up.
At last, able to ask
the doctor about a small thing,
I wonder why each morning
my eyes refuse to open.
'That is called dry eye,'
she said, and now I have
a bottle of borrowed tears
to irrigate my orbs.
Meanwhile my blood moves,
my breast makes liquid food,
my mouth is able to make
a comfortable swamp
for my damp tongue.
It's just the eyes
refusing to comply,
to watch or even weep,
retiring to some desert
of their own,
until despair is fully routed,
until they're sure
your cancer's gone.

Years

Years coil up
like dormant snails,
waiting for the rain.
Then, like a storm
unleashing
its pent up erosion,
our real ages
find us, and delve in.

Words come – since
I had the children,
since your radiation –
seam, flake, loosen, striate;
belly, lip, eyes, neck.

We are submitting
to a new dress code;
inside, outraged.

Retail Therapy

When we were courting,
we loved to go shopping,
everything he tried on looked well,
as a clothes-horse he's a natural,
with his long athletic limbs,
and excellent proportions.

Now I'm off on a solo quest,
ready to pounce on turquoise and lace,
escaping the August drizzle.
Around me women are fingering
the ruches and ruffles on the rails,
eyes glazed with late afternoon fatigue
and bargain overwhelm.
We're all sorts, from plump to gaunt,
me determined that middle-age
won't forbid me the footless tights
the sales lady says are all the rage
'with the girls' these days.

I bring home my haul
of pretty skirts I might wear
once or twice in the coming year.
My comfortable jeans
are flung back on, and the evening
unfolds with feeding, cleaning, play,
TV, books and bed; me falling asleep
between two snoring golden heads.

He never liked to spend on clothes,
so it was hard for me to wheedle
the cash out of him to actually buy
the swanky shirts and trews
he modelled for me in the dressing-room.

Now he's paying hand over fist
for potions and remedies,
to shrink the anarchic spread
returning to infest his throat.
As I doze upstairs he pads the kitchen,
revolving between doses, gargling and mixing
in a tightening circle of self-help.

This sickness brings the hero out in him;
in me, the shrew – I have few noble feelings left.
I hoard my bags of summer finery
that will fail to hide my saggy middle or big legs:
I curdle in my healthiness
downing chocolate and beer,
like it was my last elixir,
like it was me who needed a raft.

Hallowe'ened

Lurking in his throat,
The Thing hungers to lick
the last of our festive bowl,
to wizen and warp; to strangulate.
The doctors tried to burn It out,
but It crept back, rank and gluttonous;
they wanted then a cutting spree,
but could offer little guarantee
of The Thing not clawing back.
He eschewed their knives
and figured out his own regime,
an armoury of herbal potions,
oxygen and fresh veg.
But The Thing is stoical, and now
scorns Its habitual preference
to remain invisible, spreading
an ugly trail of scales,
a dragonish infiltrator
flickering audaciously
in his longsuffering mouth.
So when he strolls in naked
from the shower – all muscled
in fitness and firm flesh, but
wearing a skull mask on his face –
I'm not ready to be Hallowe'ened,
I shiver at this Death's Head,
how its tongue speaks.

Mission

Leaping across icy canyons,
my son flies,
fearless in his cape –
he has a mission
to rescue the needy:
his father, shivering
in the frozen steppes;
his mother, locked out
on a bitter night.
Shouting as he leaps
over the savage rocks
of our sofa, he shines
in the rare joint spotlight
of two parental eyes.
Other times, he negotiates
the tightrope between us.

Dyno-Rod

I push plates of broccoli,
stuff the juicer with celery
carrot, tufts of wheatgrass,
flourishing a full glass
like a triumphant cocktail waitress.
He is dismissive:
too busy getting the shakes
from B17 doses; clearing mucous;
and I wonder if this is just
the on-off cold we've endured
all winter, or signs of worse:
I swear his breathing's thickened
and he's coughing more;
at night he's snoring louder.
But his days are still filled
with work and research:
we hold tight to rituals
like cranky crustaceans
who cannot bear
to shuck our shells.

Finally I give in
to a Gulf Stream of relent –
I shelve the veg,
and my teacherish tirade.
Instead I do the woman thing:
offer praise for a pipe well drained –
he supervised the smelly job,
chatting cheerily
to the sullen man from Dyno-Rod.
'We just need a dyno rod
for my deaf ear,' he jokes.

I laugh and let it go:
the need to control;
I let the after all,
so humdrum idea
of his death, sneak closer,
and warm itself
like a stray at the hearth.

Lucky

'I'm not lucky,'
wails my daughter,
her golden hair
spangled over my knees.
'I'm never the star at school,
never!'

No matter, I pat her head,
and stroke the soft shoulder.
'You are lucky,' I intone,
a mantra I wish her to keep
all the years in her scope:
'so beautiful, and clever,
with all the food you want,
when others are hungry.
You can draw, and read
and rollerskate, ride your bike
and see your friends.
You have a new kitten.'

I do not say
the luck is dwindling
for Zoe, our old cat,
still pretty with her butterfly ears,
the wistful, defiant slant
of her green eyes;
nor do I complain
about her father's
stealthy cancer
that has returned.

My daughter sinks her cheek
into the pillow of my thigh.

She knows that Zoe will soon die,
that life is patterned
with complexity, like
why her father is so thin,
and does not hear her calling him,
and why she finds herself
turning on her brother
in a jealous huff.

Finally she sleeps,
I relish her cosy breath
before rousing my limbs
for the downstairs scene:
time to administer
a dose of feline medicine.
I lift the soft-bellied old lady cat –
all her dignity and trust –
into my fleecy chest.

My love sits reading,
his face beneath the lamp,
so weary in repose –
yet for him, my hands
are empty. He lifts
a beckoning eye,
his cheeks kindling a smile –

a gesture from the boat
he steers on the element
of his illness,
into the teeth of chance.

Shirts

How cheering
to hang them up
billowing in April wind,
their damp creases fattening
with the scent of Spring,
how hungrily I sniff
the fragrant life in them.

He is now so thin,
nesting in the shadows
of shirts that are too big,
smelling of winter and ashes.

Surgery

The plumber says he doesn't trust cuts:
he's seen it in the pipes and boilers
of his trade – how, once the saw intrudes
the pristine insides are soiled with rust.

Operation

In the hospital,
gowned in gauzy cloth,
he is prepped;
his limbs so thin,
his head bursting with the tumour,
with knowing that wrestling
the thing out may kill him.

All day the cutters and stitchers
are at work, slicing from lip
to clavicle, sawing bone,
careful not to snick an artery,
gouging a flap from his thigh
to patch the gap
where the tumour hid
thriving in its secret lair.

When it's out –
and they have fixed the jaw
with a steel plate;
rivetted the long L-shape
of the wound –
he lies arrayed
with tubes and drains.
He floats in the shallows
of the anaesthetic,
his breath echoing eerily
from the hole in his throat,
his face utterly still.

The night before the operation
he read *Peter Pan*
to our children,

and in the morning
he surrendered;
waving from the trolley,
as if to clutch a last particle
of the life we figured for him,
as if to let it fall.

Marked

Although there was no death,
she was marked,
like the pillow,
stained with the blood
from his mouth.
The threat of it,
a ragged sound in her ears,
of crows, waiting in the trees.
He put his head –
scarred and suffering, but alive –
out of the tide of the fear;
she watches as his body,
a frail stick determined to breathe,
hauls itself into the lifeboat
of summer: warm blue evenings,
and spoons and spoons
of soft food.
It is as though the drama
is happening far away,
at the other end of a telescope,
while she curls in his unused grave
where there is nothing to say.
It is calm and safe there
anyway.

Lips

Swollen slabs, bloody and cracked –
when they open,
an unrecognisable sound comes out.
She shakes her head and cries aloud.
How can they belong to her father,
still wearing his navy Crocs,
his familiar head topped
with the same grey curls, his blue eyes
like contented fish in the twin bowls
of his spectacles?
No, she will not look, and with her brother
attempts to cram herself
under her mother's coat.
'Until Dad's lips are normal,' she decrees,
'I don't want to see him in the hospital.'

He patrols the corridor,
pushing the feeding station
that funnels food up his nostril.
The sound of wheels on the floor
is loud in the silence of the children
huddled behind their mother.

The wheels stop.
He fondles their heads.
They do not look up.

Four

When my son is grown
one day he will tell his lover –
as they swap memories,
underneath the covers –
of how when he was four
he lay in a large bed
with his sister and mother.

He asked why
his father couldn't come in –
he said: 'There's room
in this bed for Dad.'
Mum's face closed – snap –
and that was that.

When Dad did join them
ready to listen at story time –
he was too hot, and
dozed into a heavy lump.
He hated saying it –
Dad's poor neck
was sore and cut –
but he was burning up:
'Get out Dad, you're boiling.'
Dad – groggy, clumsy –
staggered into the dark.

He would hear Dad
snoring In the next room,
stuffed like an oversized doll
into the bunkbed.

Left to themselves,
it was cool again.
Mum finished the usual witch story,
he snuggled next to her soft leg,
and felt sleep come.

Falling

This business of falling out of love
is long and grim, unlike the falling in.
It has no name, drifts around our house
getting in the way. It is the guest
we can't recall inviting –
that we hope will leave, but never does.
Massively inconvenient,
it impedes our chores –
and is ignored by everyone else.
I've tried guilt-tripping myself,
but love won't come back
on my command. I've come to this truce
of knowing, yet the wrestling goes on.
How could I have been so careless?
To lose love like a fondled coin,
let it roll away and disappear,
never to be found again?
I woke one day to realise that love
like a jumper with a frayed end,
had snagged and ravelled
on so many hooks it was just
a tangled heap of yarn.
I thought I fed love well,
but somehow it starved away.
I can itemise the points
where the torrent began to fail,
or reason that here
in this house of warmth and birth
love must always prevail,
but the knowledge does not go away.
I must be smaller than I hoped,
with a heart like a worn out Valentine,
the ink bled dry. Ah, I suppose
it is just another old tale.

The Electrician Says

That he has nine children:
one disabled, one a girl,
and a wife diabetic.
That his father was disinherited –
for love – that this new lark
of working for himself
has failed to thrive.
And yes, he knows what it's like,
living with illness
and hospital visits.
All the caring
he's done for his son,
the injections. And can he
come up this evening to get paid,
as it's nearly the end of the month?

Taxi

The driver curtails
his own story of no work,
and a broken marriage, he *has* to know
why I'm going to the hospital.

A meeting with the doctor,
I divulge, to ask how long
before the cancer wins.

The driver changes tack,
reveals his other tale of loss,
a sister, dead at 43,
leaving four teenagers.

Mine are younger, I reply,
and their father does not want
a judgment of what time he's left,
would be horrified to think
I'm doing this behind his back.

We pull up at the Eye and Ear,
the driver insists on half fare:
his kind voice crumbles my step
into a wobble at the threshold.

The verdict is a year,
the consultant pats my hand.
Now I dissolve: this careful man
has never yet been wrong.

I bawl and stagger as his nurse,
smiling in her daisy white,
leads me gently to the stairs.

Between the lot of them
I can't stop,
the so long stopped up tears.

Wedding

'Hasty,' the judge mocked
until he read the letter
from the consultant,
his jaded face changing to pity.
We got the green light then,
to marry in a hurry.

We turned up in our jeans
and limped through the ceremony –
upsetting the officiating lady,
determined to make this
a special occasion.

Outside the registry office
we inked a shadow
on the next couple:
the bride, glowing in her plumage,
her robust young groom,
their flower girls fidgeting.

My brother and his wife
had used their lunch hour
to be our witnesses.
They went back to work,
and my new spouse
rode off on his bike:
the big triumph that,
with six months to live,
he could still cycle.

I had to collect our children –
the paltry nuptials would have been
disappointing – no frocks, no fun –

just this boring signing thing,
and so I kept it secret,
left them with Gran.

I sloped off to the train.
It was bright, a May day,
and I was forty-seven –
finally, improbably –
a married woman.

The Pinning

The flies are coupled
on the stationary windscreen
in hot September sun;
calm in their lust,
unfazed by his regard.

In the cleft
of an outdoor chair,
a spider huddles
over white laced eggs;
refusing to move
as I manoeuvre
with a spoon.

Just as the spiders
will hatch and catch
the progeny
of amorous flies,
one day he'll fail to move
the ragged breath
in and out of his lungs.

Meanwhile he remains
dozing in the car,
in its warm, stale fold,
tired after day hospice.
He wakes to watch the flies,
how carelessly, inevitably
the pursuit goes on:
the pinning baby-making
that – not so many years ago –
impelled him to find me.

Away

I listen
to the clean sound of wind:
I am North, far away.

The children will wake
without my warm body
to pillow their morning.
They will yawn,
their pink bodies stretching.
My mother will look at my list,
give them milk; juice; cereal,
prepare the food they like for school.
She will make them laugh,
and take them in her turquoise van
to where the other children
spill out of cars,
bags humped on their backs,
moving in waves
to desks, teachers, displays.

Rocked in the wind
the harboured boats
thrum in the sea:
a high humming tune.

Here there is no coughing man,
streaked with phlegm,
sleeping sitting up,
in his makeshift kitchen cot,
nursing his fetid wound.

The wind scoured my night clean:
caught in its song
I could not think or dream.

The Kitchen

With every portion of food we guzzle
we swell with the taint of the graveyard,
and when we laze, we arrange ourselves
around stained tissues, bottles of pills,
his lank skeletal frame.
The worst is when his neck scarf
is discarded to release the tumour,
pitted and crusted, reeking:
a hideous death flower.

Still the children manage
to laugh and leap and play:
dress ups and battles,
petting the preening cats;
settling at last
with the Disney comforts
of the screen.

Volcano

Saucer-sized homunculus
leaks scarlet pus, stains shirts,
emits an overpowering stink.

Its cousins are hidden–
their growth easier to ignore –
their plans mysterious.

This one is grumbling,
we've been warned:
it could erupt.

I have the blanket ready
for the lava burst,
and, for him, a sedative.

A quick death,
this threatened haemorrhage.
He welcomes it.

But our living memory
would be forever branded
with that surge of gore.

That's why, mornings,
I check the scene,
before I let the children in.

His Last Winter

Where the walls drip,
small birds find ways to forage –
the thaw does not extend
beyond the ivy overhang,
the skirts of stout bushes.

Elsewhere the ice tightens its hold,
and the breath freezes in the throat.

Their Side

He breathes in a guttural rasp,
all the hollows in his throat
like little devouring mouths.
For years he was immersed
in the tantalising secrets
of his family's past.
The lost ancestors clamour,
wishing to greet him,
charmed by his attention.
It won't be long now
before he joins their side
and the shadows
of their forgotten lives
will be transfigured,
into light.
It won't be long now
before he leaves us –
his living family – behind.

'Will You Be There?'

(for Pippa Donovan)

In his Christmas list my son asks Santa
'please take my Daddy's cancer lump away'.
I make apologies in advance –
Santa is the man for toys, not cures –
while wondering how to introduce
the idea of death, when a gift arrives,
a story about Old Badger, going down
a shadowy tunnel towards a light.

This helps, as I've dismissed heaven,
and fumbled the vagaries of reincarnation.
We have a new discussion
about people who have died for a while,
remembering darkness
giving way to phosphorescence,
full of family and friends.

My boy blurts: 'When I die,
and I go down the tunnel,
will you be there, Mum, in that room,
waiting for me?'

Making the Call

The snow fell like a shroud
as he slept over his soup,
the sixth day
of glaciered roads,
the car useless,
the children stranded
at my mother's.

I trudged down the hill
seeking quiche in the village,
panting home to whizz it smooth
for the sake of a few
pained, attempted swallows.

I renewed the dressing
on his suppurating tumour,
the house was humming
like a cruise ship,
with the heating full on
hour after hour, to try
and keep him warm.

It was when blood
spooled out of his mouth
and he couldn't get up
that I made the call.

The ambulance was like
a fat yellow duck, waddling
slow and sure to our door,
never slipping once
on the black ice,
nurse and driver beaming
through the blizzard.

Safe in the hospice
he looked out on the garden,
huge snowflakes circling down,
his face spreading a smile,
ready for rice pudding.

'What Can I Give Him?'

('In the Bleak Midwinter', Christina Rossetti)

She sings with rare confidence –
this red-cheeked girl out of a fairytale,
sweet mouth and yellow tumbled locks,
performing for her father,
rheum-eyed in the hospice chair.

Adrift in our own mid-winter,
the grip of fear holds general
in our land, so lately garlanded
with easy largesse, now gaunt with debt,
and the worst freeze in years.

In this place of death,
where his room is empty
of all he has been forced to shed,
and he is simply grateful for each breath,
we have this lift: our shy daughter
ablaze in song – and he sits easy:
at last, a gift he can receive.

The Closing

The children nest in the big bed,
the little one with his sweet ears
and his blonde sister snuggled close.
What is coming rages in the wind
these times of defying; of giving in.

How will it come, and can we bear
the guilt of our continued living?

In that brutal forward motion of survivors
we intend to discard his death: to thrive.

At Least

He died alone, asleep,
as I was speeding
through grey streets,
through gouts of slush,
my breath bursting
as his stopped.
Easy to run to him then,
to take his still warm hand
that would never hold mine again.

We told ourselves –
I and the gentle nurses –
that at least
it was peaceful,
and there was no pain.

Regalia

In your red shirt
and the German jacket with a swing –
both favourites for playing cello in –
you could be a soldier
laid out in his regalia.
The pinched silence
of your scarred, tucked visage
belies the smiley man you were,
revelling in music, food and wine.
Army wounds and combat
belong to your father's past.
I mocked you after my labour
of pushing out our baby,
claiming childbirth
was as tough as soldiery,
and what would you know of that?

Yet a soldier you became
to battle the invader in your throat.
You showed such strength –
the strategy and hope
leading to your master stroke –
convincing yourself
there was no real foe.
The many ambushes
took you by surprise
and wore you down.
Unfailingly stoic and benign
you were killed in action.

An incongruous widow
I am awarded,
in this bland beige room,

a no-man's-land
of simplicity.
I gaze at your profile
and oddly neatened hair:
finally, here,
you resemble
the father you revered.

Off Duty

Is my face just right,
am I looking as a widow should?
I pass the funeral parlour
where four weeks ago
the ceremony unfurled.
Now I'm laughing with the children.
The director of the solemn place
is lolling out front, sucking on a cigarette.
We exchange hellos,
and I blush, remembering
how I still haven't paid the bill,
how I nearly left that day
with someone else's flowers.

Widow

I spend a lot of time
with a smile
stretched across the chasm
of my face;
like one of those outcast chimps
who grins too much –
teeth bared in a rictus
of placate.

Erstwhile

(i.m. Peter Troop)

What if the drying edges of the leaves of memory
are in my DNA? My grandmother's recipes, her letters
and diaries, filled with what must be saved –
yet when she died her great brain was pocked
like her colander, the past leaking away,
a few memories remained:
milk in a bucket, a holiday lake.

Then it was her son's turn,
his lawyer's mind and determined tongue –
that taught me the word 'erstwhile' –
unravelling.

My memory
is a sack of seeds
the birds have pecked through –
as I carry, I feel the spill
runnelling out of my hold.

Will the swinging doors
of my crammed house
let it all blow?

Glenageary Sorting Office

I found our postman
on duty in the Sorting Office.
I hadn't spotted him in years:
assumed he'd retired.
But when I greeted:
'Long time no see,'
he smiled – his grey head
lined, but not defeated –
'I've only gone inside,' he said.
They know the markers
of our lives, these men
who bring the birthday cards,
the cards for the dead.
It made me refigure
my own trajectory: like him,
I haven't disappeared –
I contain it all:
the clamour of the babies
and the silence
of the funerals.
And now, to get things sorted
I've gone inside.

Mourning

The difference between dead
and gone is a dark hustle
of days passing, his watch
still ticking on alone.
I can feel the heat of him near –
how long is it now?
months and years:
like umbrellas inflating
and descending
move stationary.

Next Year

The gaudy leaves
are torn away,
the flesh on the fruit
succumbs to mould.
What is left – bare,
stark – an outline
for next year's
foothold.

October

Each morning the web is fanned with dew,
the circlets shining. Flies are not so plentiful,
but somehow the spinner – artful, patient –
is thriving. Splayed across my wing mirror
her trap is slung. By day she hides in a crack,
kept back by the speed of the moving car.
Pouched and buffeted, her perfect filigree
eventually frays, no use for netting food.
But each night she pulls from her unfed body
fresh gossamer, wheeled and laced
by her exact crawl, scuttle and measure,
spreading her canopy – delicate and braced.

Familiar

Nine thousand years ago
a man – or what passed then
as human – preferred
to be interred with his.
We have the bones.
Was it a lynx,
all feathery ears and grace?
or a fishing cat,
tabby and fierce?

Now some sad boy
is wondering
how to torture
a ginger tom,
how to trap and burn
a mother tortoiseshell.
Hell to pay
for any black feline.

My son whimpers,
fever simmers.
Beside him curls
his familiar –
once a kitten
cupped in his hand –
now, long and sleek,
claws – sharp as a snow leopard's –
sheathed. Five years
they've shared,
loyal as brothers.

From the tufted throat:
the throttle of a purr.
From my red-cheeked son:
the silence of tears, drying up.

Stress Buster

(for Felix)

A morning of temper
as we queue for our
long haul flight,
hoping to arrive in time,
because his granny's dying.
I have spent hours
leaning into the jaws
of suitcases or sinks,
so I've no appetite
for goonish jokes.
We crawl through
the humiliating portals
of trans-Atlantic officialdom,
and all the while,
like rose petals or cherry blossom,
wherever he can reach,
his kisses fall
upon my arm.

Winter Heroes

It comes to this:
a frozen Sunday
and a team of six.
We almost miss it
because I'm lost –
sleep deprived,
cursing soccer –
navigating Drimnagh.

How he races,
across the field –
this boy who's honed his skills,
suffered snubs, misses,
injuries, lumpy pitches,
slanted goalposts
and biased refs.
Once he's positioned
the stalled game
can proceed.

It's Cabo vs Bosco,
bony knees and green socks,
parents going mental
in the raw glare and gusts.
His team whirlwinds
through mucky tackles,
the lack of subs,
the unfair penalties,
studs hammering
across the turf.

Winter heroes, these:
outnumbered, away,
they take the game: 4:3.

Wash

My daughter's eyes have shrunk from all her crying,
the tears have washed her inside out.
She cannot say her reasons
as I with my cruel visor interrogate;
scolding that her see-saw moods irritate.
Still, she turns to me her too-white face,
falling on her mother's breast:
although I'm a thorny nest,
just now I'm all she's got.

The Cough

I listen.
I do not underestimate
a cough that lasts,
with no explanation.
Years I listened
for her father's cough;
his dying breaths.
And now it returns,
hungry to conquer
a new throat.
On and on
she gives herself
to the cough.
Like she is asking
to be taken to the place
her father went.
She misses him.
Does she miss him enough?
The cough is pleased
with the new host.
It stays, a week, a month,
hour after hour.
Her face grows pale,
her shoulders hunch,
her eyes are dull.
Back to the doctor I crawl,
back to pills, potions, sprays,
the suggestions of strangers;
the little I can give
with my own small hands.

My harsh face
as inside, I fall.

Doors

Our children are our legends.

EAVAN BOLAND

The room of salt
claims her
in crusted white
and subterranean blue:
my tender-cheeked girl
frosted into effigy.
Shuffling in ice dust,
I crunch through
to pull her free.
Lips puckered in salt,
we move like blind yetis
towards a spring sky, a red car,
the calling of passers-by,
the opening of doors
with their come-hither songs.

50

You're an owl from your raptor
talons to your huge eyes...

JO SHAPCOTT

My daughter grows in beauty,
mocking my lost bounty.
But in my face
with its folds and veins,
I find a tensile frame
absent from the dreamy,
pretty portraits of me, young.

As my own mother
relished mine, and willingly let go
her claim; I feast
on my girl's rising cream:
how it must become her
for the proper time.

I leave down
what often felt
a burden –

so that I can hunt,
so that I can fly.

Millefeuille

Many petalling into herself
my daughter has enough
to be contending with –
but men in offices
plot to woo her distrust:
you are *not* a flower
they tell her, you are hairy,
dirty, you have flesh
in the wrong places;
you are a vehicle
we need to overhaul:
too slow, too dull;
not shiny, not cool
– and you *smell*.

They need their wages –
who will pay? Me,
with the small money
I give her – that's their hope.
Meanwhile they cajole
a model to do their work –
bamboozling my girl
to buy the lying layers
she does not need.
She is already
a vision of beauty,
rumpled in her fleecy pjs.

The model girl
will get a cut
of what her bosses extort
from my pocket.

Hence her glazed look
of having swallowed
a smug secret.
She is the traitor cow,
who is allowed to live,
if she will lure her sisters
up the plank
to the abbatoir.

Humpty Dumpty

The red spills out of her,
my nymph daughter;
while I grow barren:
bald and shivering
between the blasts.
It suits me, this gathering in
of myself. But I hate to see
my pain live again
in her, the crunch
as her system gets going
for an over-efficient process
that will last forty years.
She might bear two babies.
Maybe none.
She still likes puppies and cartoons,
Santa; my knee.

The Tooth Fairy's Last Visit

I wait until the breath slows –
it's later now she's 13 –
then creep in on hands and knees.
I harvest her last baby tooth:
she still believes in me.
This molar is hard and clean,
it took several shots
of anaesthetic
to numb her mouth
and an implement
like a pliers to pinch it out.

I fall asleep to memories
of her merry infant years
before she stumbles to my bed,
claiming she's sick.
She grabs the duvet for herself.

My last offering, payment
for the childhood
she shared with me,
waits beneath her pillow
in her empty room.
She chose the pink and purple stripes,
the turquoise floor I painted,
her flower light still warm,
shining on the eyes
of piles of staring toys.

Cusp

The summer comes
when she can't hide
among the small flat girls.
She must emerge:
tall, womanly; ready for secondary.
She needs a talisman of dad,
so we find an old video
where the two of them dance.
She's seven, showing off
her Irish steps. Gallant,
but pale, he sways to trad
– his least favourite music –
and he holds her hand in his.

Foundation

They've already forgotten
the kangaroo story, the dog puzzle,
the farmer and the cow.
I need to remind them now
of the zoo train drawings,
the twelve days of Christmas,
our cats when they were kittens.
I wanted them to have
a solid base to step off from
into their unknown future lives.
I mixed and poured and laid,
I guarded it, and still
carry out routine inspections,
plan annual improvements
with new ingredients:
the soccer club; baking apple pie,
splashing in lakes and seas –
not forgetting the old favourite:
reading aloud at night.

Whether, later, they will even wish
to recollect the daily parts compacted there –
who knows? And I must be ready
not to care.

Deeper

(for Catherine Nunes)

We go to the edge:
we are fresh, ready
for the lacy buffeting waves,
toes gripping shingle.

While our daughters squat on sand
immersed in shell games,
the tide swallows our ankles,
hungers around our legs.

Eyes on the horizon as we wade,
we know that one by one,
our heads will disappear – already
we have seen our mothers drown.

We spend calm days avoiding stings,
nursing hurts, judging and forgiving
our faults. The sky is still a canopy
our faces can enjoy.

When the breakers fall, we stretch
to lift each other clear,
calling: 'Sister, I am here –
I am still here.'

Snowdrops

Snowdrops push
slim green helmets
through clogged leaves
and ragged nettles.
It took a while
for my addled eyes
to find their spears –
only when I turned away,
an opalescent flash
pulled me back.

It's been a bit of a struggle
they seemed to say,
what with the rain,
the weeds, and all.
But we haven't given up
just yet.

Rue des Ursins, Paris

(for Rosita)

We take the turn
not featured on the map,
where the island
meets the bridge:
we find stained glass,
a buttress of centurion wood,
and the gleaming heads
of the two bears,
fountaining just for us
the sound of water
in this sunken street,
scented with lavender,
all bustle snuffed,
where no sign led –
simply our noses.

Benchmark

Green tufts at my toes,
I rest on slats of wood
in this garden sweet spot,
where the sun lands,
and there's no taunting breeze.
Scents of orange and rose
waft over my shoulder,
earwigs and spiders weave
their small journeys
through the twining grass.
Pigeons croon, a blue tit
darts to the feeder for a feast.
As I sit in the cradling heat,
I recall his scrawny, dying body,
how, on fine days,
he'd push the mower
a length or two, and finish
with a sunbath on this bench:
the pale face covered in a beard,
throat swathed with a scarf,
eyes shrunk shut.
He was soaking that time
into himself, that short quiet treat
in his private, untold hell

Witness

I have my dead, and I have let them go,
and was amazed to see them so contented...

RILKE

The dead must know our love,
even though we fear they left in doubt.
We sit in the silence
of their cooling limbs,
thinking our presence wasted,
watching their stiff faces,
afraid, yet hopeful that a brow
might twitch and their lips open,
whispering 'it's all a mistake'.
As they settle into their new state
of cadaver, some essence remains,
and we crave its forgiveness,
the invisible heart of a burning flame.

August

(West Pier, Dun Laoghaire)

Dip your hand into the water:
it is warm. Our red and yellow craft,
small tippy kayaks, quiver
to swiftness with a few
deft paddles, swerving
between the big boats.
A seal's head surfaces
all whiskers and liquid eyes,
then dives. The pier walls loom,
trailing weedpods.
Walkers plonk there
far from our slimline grace.
After the lesson we roll
right into the water,
bobbing in our sleek suits
as the sea reclaims our limbs,
as the sky lowers
its soft evening.